Table of Contents

Chapter 1: Introduction to AI Technical Program Management

The Role of an AI Technical Program Manager

The role of an AI Technical Program Manager is crucial in the development and implementation of AI projects within an organization. This individual is responsible for overseeing the technical aspects of AI initiatives, coordinating teams of data scientists, engineers, and other professionals, and ensuring that projects are completed on time and within budget. The AI Technical Program Manager must possess a strong technical background in AI and machine learning, as well as excellent project management skills.

One of the key responsibilities of an AI Technical Program Manager is to develop and maintain project plans that outline the scope, timeline, and resources required for AI projects. This individual must work closely with stakeholders to understand their requirements and expectations, and then translate these into actionable project plans. The AI Technical Program Manager is also responsible for monitoring progress, identifying and resolving issues, and communicating updates to stakeholders.

In addition to project management, the AI Technical Program Manager plays a critical role in driving innovation within the organization. This individual must stay up-to-date on the latest advancements in AI and machine learning technologies, and identify opportunities to apply these innovations to improve business processes and drive competitive advantage. The AI Technical Program Manager must also foster a culture of continuous learning and improvement within the AI team, encouraging team members to pursue professional development opportunities and expand their skills.

To excel in the role of an AI Technical Program Manager, individuals must possess a unique combination of technical expertise, project management skills, and leadership abilities. They must be able to communicate effectively with both technical and non-technical stakeholders, and have a strong understanding of the business implications of AI initiatives. Additionally, AI Technical Program Managers must be able to adapt to rapidly changing environments and navigate complex organizational structures to drive successful project outcomes.

In conclusion, the role of an AI Technical Program Manager is multifaceted and requires a diverse skill set to be successful. By mastering the technical aspects of AI, developing strong project management skills, and fostering a culture of innovation within the organization, individuals can position themselves for success in this exciting and rapidly growing field. For professionals looking to advance their careers in AI, becoming an AI Technical Program Manager offers a rewarding and challenging opportunity to make a significant impact in the world of artificial intelligence.

Why Pursue a Career in AI Technical Program Management

As the field of artificial intelligence continues to grow and evolve, there is an increasing demand for professionals who can manage complex AI projects and programs. This is where AI technical program managers come in. These professionals play a crucial role in overseeing the development and implementation of AI systems, ensuring that they meet the needs of both the business and the end users.

One of the main reasons to pursue a career in AI technical program management is the exciting and rapidly evolving nature of the field. AI technology is constantly advancing, and there are always new challenges and opportunities to be tackled. As an AI technical program manager, you will have the chance to work on cutting-edge projects and help shape the future of AI technology.

Another reason to consider a career in AI technical program management is the potential for career growth and advancement. As AI becomes increasingly integrated into businesses across all industries, the demand for skilled AI technical program managers is only expected to increase. This means that there will be ample opportunities for advancement and career development in this field.

Additionally, pursuing a career in AI technical program management can be financially rewarding. AI technical program managers are highly sought after and command competitive salaries. With the right skills and experience, you can expect to earn a lucrative salary and enjoy a rewarding career in this field.

Overall, for professionals who are passionate about AI technology and are looking for a challenging and rewarding career, pursuing a career in AI technical program management can be a great choice. With the right skills, experience, and dedication, you can become a successful AI technical program manager and play a key role in shaping the future of AI technology.

Chapter 2: Understanding Artificial Intelligence

Basics of Artificial Intelligence

Artificial Intelligence, or AI, is a rapidly growing field that is revolutionizing the way we live and work. In order to become an AI Technical Program Manager, it is essential to have a solid understanding of the basics of AI. This subchapter will provide an overview of the fundamental concepts and principles of artificial intelligence that every aspiring AI Technical Program Manager should be familiar with.

One of the key concepts in AI is machine learning, which is a subset of AI that allows machines to learn from data without being explicitly programmed. Machine learning algorithms can analyze large amounts of data to identify patterns and make predictions. As an AI Technical Program Manager, it is important to understand how machine learning works and how it can be applied to solve real-world problems.

Another important concept in AI is neural networks, which are a type of machine learning algorithm inspired by the structure of the human brain. Neural networks consist of interconnected nodes, or neurons, that process information and make decisions. Understanding how neural networks work is crucial for developing AI applications that can perform complex tasks such as image recognition and natural language processing.

In addition to machine learning and neural networks, AI Technical Program Managers must also be familiar with other AI techniques such as natural language processing, computer vision, and reinforcement learning. Natural language processing allows computers to understand and generate human language, while computer vision enables machines to interpret and analyze visual information. Reinforcement learning is a type of machine learning algorithm that learns through trial and error, making decisions to maximize rewards.

Overall, a solid understanding of the basics of artificial intelligence is essential for anyone looking to become an AI Technical Program Manager. By mastering the fundamental concepts and principles of AI, aspiring AI Technical Program Managers can develop the knowledge and skills needed to lead AI projects and teams effectively. With the rapid advancement of AI technology, staying up-to-date on the latest developments in the field is also crucial for success in this dynamic and exciting field.

Applications of AI in Various Industries

Artificial intelligence (AI) has revolutionized various industries by automating tasks, improving efficiency, and enabling businesses to make data-driven decisions. In this subchapter, we will explore the applications of AI in various industries and how it has transformed the way businesses operate.

One of the industries that has significantly benefited from AI is healthcare. AI-powered applications are being used to diagnose diseases, personalize treatment plans, and improve patient outcomes. For example, AI algorithms can analyze medical images to detect abnormalities with higher accuracy than human radiologists. AI is also being used to predict patient outcomes and recommend personalized treatment plans based on a patient's unique health data.

Another industry that has embraced AI is finance. AI-powered algorithms are being used to detect fraudulent transactions, optimize trading strategies, and predict market trends. Banks and financial institutions are using AI to automate customer service, streamline loan approval processes, and personalize financial advice for customers. AI is also being used to analyze vast amounts of financial data to identify investment opportunities and risks.

The retail industry has also seen significant advancements in AI technology. AI-powered recommendation engines are being used to personalize the shopping experience for customers by suggesting products based on their browsing history and preferences. Retailers are using AI to optimize pricing strategies, forecast demand, and improve inventory management. AI is also being used to automate customer service through chatbots and virtual assistants, improving customer satisfaction and reducing response times.

In the manufacturing industry, AI is being used to optimize production processes, predict equipment failures, and improve quality control. AI-powered robots are being used to automate repetitive tasks, increasing efficiency and reducing the risk of human error. Manufacturers are using AI to analyze production data in real-time, identify bottlenecks, and optimize workflows. AI is also being used to predict maintenance needs and schedule repairs before equipment failures occur, reducing downtime and increasing productivity.

In conclusion, AI is transforming various industries by automating tasks, improving decision-making, and enhancing efficiency. Professionals who want to become AI Technical Program or Project Managers need to have a deep understanding of AI technologies, industry-specific applications, and project management principles. By mastering AI and understanding its applications in various industries, professionals can lead successful AI projects and drive innovation in their organizations.

Chapter 3: Skills Required for AI Technical Program Managers

Technical Skills

As an AI Technical Program Manager or Project Manager, it is essential to possess a strong foundation in technical skills. These skills will enable you to effectively oversee and manage AI projects from inception to completion. In this subchapter, we will discuss the key technical skills that are necessary for success in this role.

First and foremost, a strong background in artificial intelligence and machine learning is crucial for an AI Technical Program Manager. Understanding the inner workings of AI algorithms and models will allow you to make informed decisions and provide valuable insights to your team. It is important to stay up-to-date with the latest advancements in AI technology to ensure that your projects are utilizing the most cutting-edge solutions.

In addition to AI and machine learning expertise, proficiency in programming languages such as Python, R, and Java is essential for an AI Technical Program Manager. Being able to write and understand code will enable you to communicate effectively with your team of developers and data scientists. It will also allow you to troubleshoot technical issues and provide hands-on support when needed.

Furthermore, a solid understanding of data management and analytics is crucial for success in this role. Being able to manipulate and analyze large datasets will help you identify trends and patterns that can drive strategic decision-making. Familiarity with data visualization tools such as Tableau or Power BI will also be beneficial for presenting your findings to stakeholders.

Lastly, strong project management skills are essential for an AI Technical Program Manager. Being able to create and manage project plans, allocate resources effectively, and communicate project updates to stakeholders are all key components of the role. By honing your technical skills and project management abilities, you will be well-equipped to lead successful AI projects and drive innovation in your organization.

Soft Skills

Soft skills are an essential component for anyone looking to become an AI Technical Program Manager or Project Manager. These skills are crucial for effectively managing teams, communicating with stakeholders, and ensuring the successful implementation of AI projects. In this section, we will explore some of the key soft skills that are necessary for success in this role.

One of the most important soft skills for an AI Technical Program Manager is communication. Effective communication is essential for conveying project requirements, objectives, and timelines to team members and stakeholders. It is also important for fostering collaboration and ensuring that everyone is on the same page. As an AI Technical Program Manager, you will need to be able to communicate complex technical concepts in a clear and concise manner to both technical and non-technical audiences.

Another important soft skill for an AI Technical Program Manager is leadership. As a leader, you will be responsible for guiding and motivating your team to achieve their goals. This requires strong decision-making skills, the ability to inspire others, and a willingness to take on challenges. Additionally, effective leadership involves being able to delegate tasks, provide feedback, and resolve conflicts in a constructive manner.

Problem-solving is another critical soft skill for an AI Technical Program Manager. In this role, you will be faced with a variety of challenges, from technical issues to budget constraints. Being able to think creatively and develop innovative solutions is essential for overcoming these obstacles and ensuring the success of your projects. Additionally, being able to adapt to changing circumstances and adjust your approach as needed is key to navigating the complex and ever-evolving field of AI.

Collaboration is another important soft skill for an AI Technical Program Manager. In this role, you will be working with a diverse team of individuals, including data scientists, engineers, and business stakeholders. Being able to collaborate effectively with these different groups, as well as external partners and vendors, is essential for ensuring the success of your projects. This requires strong interpersonal skills, the ability to build relationships, and a willingness to listen and consider different perspectives.

Finally, time management is a crucial soft skill for an AI Technical Program Manager. In this role, you will be responsible for overseeing multiple projects simultaneously, each with its own set of deadlines and deliverables. Being able to prioritize tasks, allocate resources effectively, and manage your time efficiently is essential for meeting project milestones and ensuring the successful completion of your projects. By developing and honing these key soft skills, you will be well-equipped to excel as an AI Technical Program Manager and lead your team to success in the dynamic and challenging field of artificial intelligence.

Project Management Skills

Project management skills are crucial for anyone aspiring to become an AI Technical Program or Project Manager. These roles require individuals to oversee complex projects involving artificial intelligence technologies, requiring a deep understanding of both AI and project management principles. To succeed in these positions, professionals must possess a range of project management skills that will enable them to effectively lead teams, manage resources, and deliver projects on time and within budget.

One of the most important project management skills for AI Technical Program or Project Managers is the ability to create and execute project plans. This involves defining project objectives, determining project scope, identifying key tasks and milestones, and creating a timeline for project completion. AI projects are often complex and require careful planning to ensure successful implementation. By mastering the skill of creating and executing project plans, AI Technical Program or Project Managers can effectively manage the various aspects of AI projects and ensure that they are completed on time and within budget.

Another essential project management skill for AI Technical Program or Project Managers is the ability to communicate effectively with team members, stakeholders, and other key project stakeholders. Effective communication is essential for ensuring that all project stakeholders are aligned on project objectives, timelines, and deliverables. AI projects often involve cross-functional teams with members from various departments and backgrounds, making clear and concise communication critical for project success. By mastering the skill of effective communication, AI Technical Program or Project Managers can build strong relationships with team members and stakeholders, foster collaboration, and ensure that everyone is working towards a common goal.

In addition to creating project plans and communicating effectively, AI Technical Program or Project Managers must also possess strong leadership skills. Leadership is essential for inspiring and motivating team members, resolving conflicts, and making difficult decisions. AI projects can be challenging and may encounter unexpected obstacles along the way. By mastering the skill of leadership, AI Technical Program or Project Managers can guide their teams through these challenges, keep team morale high, and ensure that projects stay on track.

Furthermore, AI Technical Program or Project Managers must have excellent problem-solving skills. AI projects are often complex and may require creative solutions to overcome obstacles and achieve project objectives. By mastering the skill of problem-solving, AI Technical Program or Project Managers can identify potential risks, develop contingency plans, and find innovative solutions to project challenges. This skill is essential for ensuring that AI projects are delivered successfully and that project goals are met.

In conclusion, project management skills are essential for anyone aspiring to become an AI Technical Program or Project Manager. By mastering the skills of creating and executing project plans, communicating effectively, demonstrating strong leadership, and solving problems creatively, professionals can excel in these roles and effectively manage AI projects. With the right combination of project management skills and a deep understanding of AI technologies, individuals can become successful AI Technical Program or Project Managers and lead their teams to project success.

Chapter 4: Educational Background and Certifications

Degrees in AI and Related Fields

For professionals that want to know what it will take to become an AI Technical Program or Project Manager, pursuing a degree in Artificial Intelligence (AI) or a related field is essential. In this subchapter, we will discuss the various degrees available for individuals interested in pursuing a career in AI and related fields.

One of the most common degrees for individuals interested in AI is a Bachelor's degree in Computer Science with a concentration in AI. This degree provides students with a strong foundation in computer science principles, as well as specialized coursework in AI algorithms, machine learning, and data science. Graduates with this degree are well-equipped to pursue entry-level positions in AI development and research.

For those looking to specialize further in AI, a Master's degree in AI or a related field is highly recommended. This advanced degree provides students with a deeper understanding of AI concepts and techniques, as well as the opportunity to conduct research in cutting-edge AI technologies. Graduates with a Master's degree in AI are well-positioned to pursue leadership roles in AI development and project management.

In addition to traditional degrees in Computer Science and AI, there are also specialized programs available for individuals interested in specific areas of AI, such as natural language processing, computer vision, and robotics. These programs provide in-depth training in specialized AI techniques and technologies, allowing graduates to become experts in their chosen field.

For professionals looking to advance their career in AI project management, pursuing a certification in AI project management can also be beneficial. These certifications provide individuals with the knowledge and skills needed to effectively manage AI projects, from planning and development to implementation and evaluation. By obtaining a certification in AI project management, professionals can demonstrate their expertise in this specialized area and enhance their career prospects in the field of AI.

Overall, pursuing a degree or certification in AI or a related field is essential for professionals looking to become AI Technical Program or Project Managers. By obtaining the necessary education and training, individuals can develop the skills and knowledge needed to succeed in this exciting and rapidly growing field.

Relevant Certifications for AI Technical Program Managers

Aspiring AI Technical Program Managers should consider obtaining relevant certifications to enhance their skills and credibility in the field. These certifications can demonstrate to employers and colleagues that they possess the necessary expertise and knowledge to effectively manage AI projects. Some of the most important certifications for AI Technical Program Managers include the Certified AI Professional (CAIP), Certified AI Project Manager (CAIPM), and Certified Machine Learning Engineer (CMLE).

The Certified AI Professional (CAIP) certification is designed for professionals who want to demonstrate their expertise in AI technologies and applications. This certification covers a wide range of topics, including machine learning, natural language processing, computer vision, and robotics. By obtaining the CAIP certification, AI Technical Program Managers can show that they have a comprehensive understanding of AI concepts and techniques.

Another valuable certification for AI Technical Program Managers is the Certified AI Project Manager (CAIPM) certification. This certification is specifically tailored for professionals who are responsible for managing AI projects from start to finish. The CAIPM certification covers topics such as project planning, risk management, resource allocation, and stakeholder communication. By earning this certification, AI Technical Program Managers can demonstrate their ability to successfully lead AI projects and deliver results on time and within budget.

For AI Technical Program Managers who specialize in machine learning, the Certified Machine Learning Engineer (CMLE) certification is a must-have. This certification is designed for professionals who are proficient in building and deploying machine learning models. The CMLE certification covers topics such as data preprocessing, model selection, hyperparameter tuning, and model evaluation. By obtaining the CMLE certification, AI Technical Program Managers can showcase their expertise in machine learning and their ability to develop cutting-edge AI solutions.

In conclusion, obtaining relevant certifications is essential for AI Technical Program Managers who want to advance their careers and stand out in a competitive job market. By earning certifications such as the CAIP, CAIPM, and CMLE, AI Technical Program Managers can demonstrate their expertise in AI technologies, project management, and machine learning. These certifications can help AI Technical Program Managers secure job opportunities, advance their careers, and make a meaningful impact in the field of artificial intelligence.

Chapter 5: Gaining Experience in AI

Internships and Entry-Level Positions

Internships and entry-level positions are crucial steps on the path to becoming an AI Technical Program or Project Manager. These opportunities provide valuable hands-on experience and allow you to gain insights into the industry while honing your skills. Internships also offer the chance to network with professionals in the field, which can lead to future job opportunities.

When looking for internships or entry-level positions in AI, it is important to research companies that align with your career goals and interests. Look for organizations that are at the forefront of AI technology and innovation, as these companies are more likely to provide valuable learning experiences. Additionally, consider reaching out to professionals in the industry for advice and guidance on potential opportunities.

During your internship or entry-level position, make the most of your time by actively seeking out new challenges and learning opportunities. Take on projects that allow you to apply your AI skills and knowledge, and don't be afraid to ask questions or seek guidance from more experienced team members. Building a strong foundation of practical experience is essential for advancing your career in AI.

As you gain experience through internships and entry-level positions, begin to develop a portfolio of your work to showcase your skills and accomplishments. This portfolio can include projects you have worked on, papers you have written, or any other relevant contributions to the field of AI. Having a strong portfolio will demonstrate your capabilities to potential employers and set you apart from other candidates.

Ultimately, internships and entry-level positions are stepping stones on the path to becoming an AI Technical Program or Project Manager. By actively seeking out opportunities, building a network of professionals in the industry, and continuously developing your skills and knowledge, you will be well-positioned to advance your career in AI and achieve your goals as a Technical Program Manager.

Networking in the AI Industry

Networking in the AI industry is crucial for professionals looking to advance their careers as AI Technical Program or Project Managers. Building relationships with other professionals in the field can open up new opportunities for collaboration, job prospects, and professional growth. Networking allows individuals to stay updated on the latest trends, technologies, and best practices in the AI industry, giving them a competitive edge in their careers.

One effective way to network in the AI industry is to attend industry conferences, seminars, and workshops. These events provide a great opportunity to meet and connect with other professionals in the field, as well as learn from industry experts through keynote speeches, panel discussions, and interactive sessions. By actively participating in these events, individuals can expand their knowledge, build relationships, and stay abreast of the latest developments in AI technology.

Another important aspect of networking in the AI industry is to actively engage with online communities and forums dedicated to artificial intelligence. Platforms like LinkedIn, Twitter, and specialized AI forums allow professionals to connect with like-minded individuals, share insights, and seek advice from experts in the field. By regularly interacting with these online communities, individuals can build a strong professional network that can help them in their career advancement.

In addition to attending events and engaging with online communities, professionals looking to network in the AI industry should also consider joining professional organizations and associations related to artificial intelligence. These organizations offer networking opportunities, industry insights, and resources to help individuals stay updated on the latest trends and developments in the field. By becoming a member of these organizations, professionals can connect with other industry experts, access valuable resources, and enhance their professional reputation in the AI industry.

Overall, networking in the AI industry is a key component of success for professionals looking to become AI Technical Program or Project Managers. By actively participating in industry events, engaging with online communities, and joining professional organizations, individuals can build a strong professional network, stay updated on industry trends, and create new opportunities for career advancement. Networking is not just about building connections, but also about building relationships that can help individuals thrive in the fast-paced and ever-evolving field of artificial intelligence.

Chapter 6: Transitioning to a Technical Program Manager Role

Building a Portfolio of AI Projects

Building a Portfolio of AI Projects is crucial for professionals looking to break into the field of Artificial Intelligence as a Technical Program or Project Manager. Your portfolio will showcase your skills, expertise, and experience in working on AI projects, and will set you apart from other candidates in the competitive job market. In this subchapter, we will discuss how to effectively build a portfolio of AI projects that will impress potential employers and help you land your dream job in AI.

The first step in building a portfolio of AI projects is to identify the types of projects you want to work on. This could include machine learning, natural language processing, computer vision, or any other subfield of AI that interests you. Once you have identified the types of projects you want to work on, you can start looking for opportunities to gain hands-on experience in those areas. This could be through internships, freelance projects, or even personal projects that you work on in your spare time.

Next, it's important to document your work on these projects in a way that is clear, concise, and easy to understand. This could include creating a portfolio website or blog where you showcase your projects, explaining the problem you were trying to solve, the approach you took, and the results you achieved. You should also include any code, data, or visualizations that demonstrate your skills and expertise in AI.

In addition to showcasing your technical skills, it's also important to highlight your project management skills in your portfolio. This could include detailing how you managed timelines, budgets, and resources on your projects, as well as any challenges you faced and how you overcame them. Employers are looking for AI Technical Program and Project Managers who can not only deliver high-quality AI projects, but also manage teams and stakeholders effectively.

Finally, don't be afraid to reach out to potential employers and share your portfolio with them. Networking is key in the field of AI, and building relationships with hiring managers and recruiters can help you land your dream job. By building a strong portfolio of AI projects and effectively showcasing your skills and expertise, you will be well on your way to becoming an AI Technical Program or Project Manager.

Interview Tips for AI Technical Program Manager Positions

If you are aspiring to become an AI Technical Program Manager, you must be prepared to face tough competition in the job market. To help you stand out during the interview process, here are some essential tips to keep in mind:

1. Showcase your technical expertise: As an AI Technical Program Manager, you will be expected to have a strong understanding of artificial intelligence technologies and programming languages. During the interview, be prepared to discuss your technical skills and experiences in detail. Highlight any projects you have worked on that demonstrate your knowledge and expertise in AI.

2. Demonstrate your project management skills: In addition to technical knowledge, AI Technical Program Managers must also possess strong project management skills. Be ready to discuss your experience leading cross-functional teams, managing budgets and timelines, and solving complex problems. Provide examples of successful projects you have managed in the past.

3. Highlight your communication skills: As a liaison between technical and non-technical teams, AI Technical Program Managers must have excellent communication skills. During the interview, be sure to articulate your ideas clearly and concisely. Show that you can effectively communicate complex technical concepts to a non-technical audience.

4. Be prepared to answer behavioral questions: Interviewers will likely ask you about how you have handled challenging situations in the past. Be ready to provide specific examples of times when you have successfully resolved conflicts, managed difficult stakeholders, or overcome obstacles in a project. Use the STAR method (Situation, Task, Action, Result) to structure your responses.

5. Research the company and the industry: Before your interview, take the time to research the company and the industry in which it operates. Understand how artificial intelligence is being used in that particular sector and be prepared to discuss how you can contribute to the

organization's goals. Showing that you have done your homework demonstrates your interest and commitment to the role.

By following these tips and thoroughly preparing for your interview, you can increase your chances of landing a coveted AI Technical Program Manager position. Remember to be confident, professional, and enthusiastic about the opportunity to work in the exciting field of artificial intelligence. Good luck!

Chapter 7: Advancing Your Career in AI Technical Program Management

Continuing Education and Professional Development

In the ever-evolving field of artificial intelligence (AI), it is crucial for professionals to prioritize continuing education and professional development in order to stay relevant and competitive. As an AI Technical Program or Project Manager, it is important to constantly build upon your knowledge and skills to remain at the forefront of the industry. This subchapter will explore the importance of continuing education and professional development for aspiring AI Technical Program Managers and provide guidance on how to effectively pursue further learning opportunities.

One of the key reasons why continuing education is essential for AI Technical Program Managers is the rapid pace at which technology is advancing. New developments and innovations in AI are constantly being made, and professionals must stay informed in order to effectively lead and manage AI projects. By staying up-to-date with the latest trends, tools, and techniques in AI, professionals can ensure that they are equipped to make informed decisions and drive successful outcomes for their organizations.

Professional development is also important for AI Technical Program Managers to enhance their leadership and management skills. As a manager, it is crucial to have strong communication, problem-solving, and decision-making abilities in order to effectively lead a team and deliver results. By investing in professional development opportunities such as leadership training, project management courses, and communication workshops, professionals can further develop these essential skills and become more effective leaders in the AI industry.

In addition to formal education and training, professionals can also benefit from networking and mentorship opportunities to further their career growth. Building relationships with other professionals in the industry can provide valuable insights, advice, and support. Seeking out mentors who have experience in AI Technical Program Management can also offer guidance and help professionals navigate their career path. By actively engaging in networking events, conferences, and industry meetups, professionals can expand their knowledge and connections within the AI community.

Ultimately, continuing education and professional development are essential components of a successful career as an AI Technical Program or Project Manager. By staying informed, enhancing leadership skills, and building a strong network of support, professionals can position themselves for long-term success in the rapidly growing field of artificial intelligence. By prioritizing ongoing learning and growth, professionals can stay ahead of the curve and make meaningful contributions to the advancement of AI technology.

Leadership Opportunities in the AI Industry

In the fast-evolving world of artificial intelligence (AI), leadership opportunities are abundant for professionals looking to make a mark in the industry. As an AI Technical Program Manager or Project Manager, you have the chance to drive innovation, lead cross-functional teams, and shape the future of AI technologies. In this subchapter, we will explore the various leadership opportunities available in the AI industry and what it takes to excel in these roles.

One of the key leadership opportunities in the AI industry is the chance to lead high-impact projects that leverage cutting-edge AI technologies. As an AI Technical Program Manager, you will be responsible for overseeing the planning, execution, and delivery of AI projects that have the potential to revolutionize industries. This role requires a deep understanding of AI technologies, as well as strong project management skills to ensure that projects are completed on time and within budget.

Another leadership opportunity in the AI industry is the chance to lead cross-functional teams comprised of data scientists, engineers, and other AI professionals. As an AI Technical Program Manager, you will need to leverage your communication and interpersonal skills to effectively collaborate with team members from diverse backgrounds. By fostering a culture of collaboration and innovation, you can drive your team towards achieving its goals and delivering impactful AI solutions.

In addition to leading projects and teams, AI Technical Program Managers also have the opportunity to influence strategic decision-making within their organizations. By staying abreast of the latest AI trends and developments, you can provide valuable insights and recommendations to senior leadership on how to best leverage AI technologies to achieve business objectives. This strategic leadership role requires a strong business acumen, as well as the ability to think critically and creatively about how AI can drive value for the organization.

As an AI Technical Program Manager or Project Manager, you also have the opportunity to mentor and develop the next generation of AI professionals. By sharing your knowledge and expertise with junior team members, you can help them grow and advance in their careers. This mentorship role not only benefits the individual, but also contributes to the overall success of the team and organization.

In conclusion, the AI industry offers a wealth of leadership opportunities for professionals looking to make a difference. By leveraging your technical expertise, project management skills, and strategic thinking, you can excel as an AI Technical Program Manager or Project Manager and drive innovation in this dynamic field. Whether you are leading high-impact projects, collaborating with cross-functional teams, influencing strategic decision-making, or mentoring junior professionals, there are countless ways to make your mark as a leader in the AI industry.

Chapter 8: Conclusion

Final Thoughts on Becoming an AI Technical Program Manager

As we come to the end of this guide on becoming an AI Technical Program Manager, it is important to reflect on the key takeaways and final thoughts that can help professionals navigate this exciting and rapidly evolving field. The role of an AI Technical Program Manager requires a unique blend of technical expertise, project management skills, and a deep understanding of artificial intelligence technologies. By mastering these skills, professionals can position themselves for success in this dynamic and high-demand field.

One of the most important aspects of becoming an AI Technical Program Manager is staying current with the latest advancements in artificial intelligence technologies. This field is constantly evolving, and professionals must be proactive in keeping up-to-date with new developments, trends, and best practices. By staying informed, AI Technical Program Managers can make informed decisions, drive innovation, and lead their teams to success.

In addition to technical expertise, AI Technical Program Managers must also possess strong project management skills. This includes the ability to set clear goals, create detailed project plans, manage resources effectively, and communicate with stakeholders at all levels. By honing these skills, professionals can ensure that projects are delivered on time, within budget, and with the desired outcomes.

Another key aspect of becoming an AI Technical Program Manager is building strong relationships with cross-functional teams, stakeholders, and external partners. Collaboration is essential in this role, as AI projects often involve multiple teams working together towards a common goal. By fostering a culture of collaboration and communication, AI Technical Program Managers can drive teamwork, build trust, and ensure the success of their projects.

In conclusion, becoming an AI Technical Program Manager is a challenging yet rewarding journey that requires a unique set of skills, expertise, and a passion for artificial intelligence. By mastering technical knowledge, project management skills, and the ability to collaborate effectively, professionals can excel in this dynamic and high-impact field. With dedication, perseverance, and a commitment to continuous learning, aspiring AI Technical Program Managers can make a significant impact in the world of artificial intelligence.

Resources for Further Learning and Development

In order to truly master the skills required to become an AI Technical Program Manager, it is important to continue learning and developing your knowledge in the field of artificial intelligence. There are a variety of resources available to help you further your education and advance your career in this exciting and rapidly growing industry.

One valuable resource for further learning is online courses and tutorials. Platforms such as Coursera, Udemy, and edX offer a wide range of courses in artificial intelligence, machine learning, and data science. These courses are taught by industry experts and can help you deepen your understanding of key concepts and techniques in AI.

Another valuable resource for further learning is books and academic papers. There are many excellent books on artificial intelligence and related topics that can provide in-depth knowledge and insights into the field. Some recommended books include "Artificial Intelligence: A Modern Approach" by Stuart Russell and Peter Norvig, "Deep Learning" by Ian Goodfellow, Yoshua

Bengio, and Aaron Courville, and "Pattern Recognition and Machine Learning" by Christopher Bishop.

Attending conferences and workshops is another great way to expand your knowledge and network with other professionals in the field of artificial intelligence. Events such as the Neural Information Processing Systems (NeurIPS) conference, the International Conference on Machine Learning (ICML), and the Association for the Advancement of Artificial Intelligence (AAAI) conference offer valuable opportunities to learn from leading experts and stay up-to-date on the latest developments in AI.

Networking with other professionals in the field of artificial intelligence is also a key resource for further learning and development. Joining professional organizations such as the Association for Computing Machinery (ACM) or the Institute of Electrical and Electronics Engineers (IEEE) can provide valuable networking opportunities and access to resources such as online forums, webinars, and workshops.

Finally, seeking out mentorship from experienced AI Technical Program Managers can be a valuable resource for further learning and development. A mentor can provide guidance, advice, and support as you navigate your career in AI, and can help you identify areas for growth and improvement. By taking advantage of these resources for further learning and development, you can continue to build your skills and expertise as you work towards becoming a successful AI Technical Program Manager.

Becoming an AI Technical Program Manager (AI TPM) requires a blend of technical expertise, program management skills, and knowledge specific to AI and machine learning. Here's a comprehensive list of the skills needed:

Technical Skills

1. **Understanding of AI and Machine Learning**
   - Knowledge of AI concepts, techniques, and algorithms
   - Familiarity with machine learning frameworks (e.g., TensorFlow, PyTorch)
   - Experience with data processing and analysis
2. **Software Development**
   - Proficiency in programming languages (e.g., Python, Java, C++)
   - Understanding of software development lifecycle
   - Experience with version control systems (e.g., Git)
3. **Data Management**
   - Knowledge of databases and data structures
   - Experience with data collection, cleaning, and preprocessing
   - Understanding of big data technologies (e.g., Hadoop, Spark)

Program Management Skills

1. **Project Planning and Execution**
   - Ability to create and manage project plans
   - Experience with project management tools (e.g., Jira, Trello)
   - Strong organizational skills
2. **Agile and Scrum Methodologies**
   - Understanding of Agile principles and practices
   - Experience in running Scrum meetings and sprints
3. **Risk Management**
   - Ability to identify, assess, and mitigate risks
   - Experience with contingency planning
4. **Budget and Resource Management**
   - Ability to manage project budgets

- Skill in resource allocation and optimization

Communication and Interpersonal Skills

1. **Stakeholder Management**
   - Ability to communicate effectively with stakeholders at all levels
   - Experience in managing stakeholder expectations
2. **Team Collaboration**
   - Strong teamwork and collaboration skills
   - Ability to lead cross-functional teams
3. **Conflict Resolution**
   - Ability to manage and resolve conflicts within the team
   - Strong negotiation skills

Leadership Skills

1. **Vision and Strategy**
   - Ability to define project vision and strategy
   - Experience in aligning project goals with business objectives
2. **Decision Making**
   - Strong decision-making skills
   - Ability to make data-driven decisions
3. **Motivation and Inspiration**
   - Ability to inspire and motivate the team
   - Skill in creating a positive team environment

Domain-Specific Knowledge

1. **AI Ethics and Compliance**
   - Understanding of ethical considerations in AI
   - Knowledge of compliance and regulatory requirements
2. **Industry Knowledge**
   - Familiarity with industry trends and best practices
   - Understanding of the competitive landscape

Analytical and Problem-Solving Skills

1. **Critical Thinking**
   - Ability to think critically and analytically
   - Strong problem-solving skills
2. **Data Analysis**
   - Proficiency in data analysis and interpretation
   - Experience with data visualization tools (e.g., Tableau, Power BI)

Continuous Learning and Adaptability

1. **Learning Agility**
   - Ability to quickly learn and adapt to new technologies and methodologies
   - Commitment to continuous learning and improvement
2. **Adaptability**
   - Ability to adapt to changing project requirements and environments
   - Flexibility in managing multiple priorities

Certification and Education

1. **Relevant Degrees**
   - Bachelor's or Master's degree in Computer Science, Engineering, or a related field
2. **Certifications**
   - Project Management Professional (PMP) or Agile certifications (e.g., Certified ScrumMaster)
   - AI and machine learning certifications (e.g., Coursera, edX, Udacity)

Having a combination of these skills and continually developing them will prepare you for a successful career as an AI Technical Program Manager.

Many top companies are actively hiring AI Technical Program Managers as they continue to expand their AI capabilities and projects. Here are some of the leading companies in this space:

Technology Companies

1. **Google**
   - Google AI and DeepMind divisions
   - Roles focused on machine learning, natural language processing, and AI research
2. **Microsoft**
   - Azure AI and other AI initiatives
   - Positions related to cloud-based AI services, machine learning, and AI-driven products
3. **Amazon**
   - Amazon Web Services (AWS) and Amazon AI
   - Opportunities in machine learning, AI research, and AI-based product development
4. **Apple**
   - AI and machine learning teams
   - Roles involving Siri, machine learning, and other AI-powered features
5. **Facebook (Meta)**
   - AI Research (FAIR) and applied machine learning teams
   - Positions related to social media, virtual reality, and AI-driven user experiences
6. **IBM**
   - IBM Watson and AI teams
   - Opportunities in AI-driven business solutions, machine learning, and data science
7. **Tesla**
   - Autopilot and AI teams
   - Roles focused on autonomous driving, machine learning, and AI-driven innovation

Consulting Firms

1. **Accenture**
   - AI and machine learning consulting services
   - Positions in implementing AI solutions for various industries
2. **Deloitte**
   - AI and analytics practice
   - Roles in AI strategy, implementation, and consulting
3. **PwC**
   - AI and machine learning consulting
   - Opportunities in delivering AI-driven business solutions

Healthcare and Biotech Companies

1. **Johnson & Johnson**
   - AI initiatives in healthcare and medical devices
   - Positions in AI-driven research and development
2. **Pfizer**
   - AI and machine learning teams
   - Roles in drug discovery, clinical trials, and healthcare solutions
3. **Roche**
   - AI-driven healthcare and diagnostics projects
   - Opportunities in machine learning and AI research

Automotive Companies

1. **Ford**
   - AI initiatives in autonomous driving and smart vehicles
   - Positions in AI research, machine learning, and AI-driven vehicle technologies
2. **General Motors**
   - AI and autonomous vehicle teams
   - Roles focused on machine learning, AI-driven innovation, and vehicle autonomy

Financial Services

1. **JPMorgan Chase**
   - AI and machine learning teams
   - Opportunities in AI-driven financial services and analytics
2. **Goldman Sachs**
   - AI initiatives in trading, risk management, and financial analytics
   - Roles in machine learning and AI-driven financial solutions

Startups and AI-focused Companies

1. **OpenAI**
   - AI research and development
   - Positions in cutting-edge AI research and applications
2. **Nvidia**
   - AI and machine learning hardware and software
   - Roles in developing AI-driven technologies and products
3. **UiPath**
   - AI and automation solutions
   - Opportunities in AI-driven robotic process automation

These companies are at the forefront of AI innovation and often have multiple openings for AI Technical Program Managers. Checking their careers pages, networking on LinkedIn, and staying updated with job boards are effective ways to find these opportunities.

AI Technical Program Managers are in demand across a wide range of industries due to the increasing adoption of AI technologies. Here are some of the top industries hiring for AI Technical Program Managers:

1. Technology and Software Development

- **Key Focus Areas:** AI research and development, machine learning platforms, cloud-based AI services.
- **Example Companies:** Google, Microsoft, Amazon, Apple, Facebook (Meta), IBM, Nvidia.

2. Healthcare and Biotechnology

- **Key Focus Areas:** AI-driven diagnostics, personalized medicine, drug discovery, healthcare analytics.
- **Example Companies:** Johnson & Johnson, Pfizer, Roche, GE Healthcare.

3. Financial Services

- **Key Focus Areas:** Fraud detection, risk management, trading algorithms, customer service automation.
- **Example Companies:** JPMorgan Chase, Goldman Sachs, Citibank, Wells Fargo.

4. Automotive

- **Key Focus Areas:** Autonomous driving, smart vehicles, predictive maintenance, AI-driven design and manufacturing.
- **Example Companies:** Tesla, Ford, General Motors, Waymo.

5. Retail and E-commerce

- **Key Focus Areas:** Personalized recommendations, supply chain optimization, customer service chatbots, sales forecasting.
- **Example Companies:** Amazon, Walmart, Alibaba, Target.

6. Telecommunications

- **Key Focus Areas:** Network optimization, customer service automation, predictive maintenance, AI-driven service delivery.
- **Example Companies:** AT&T, Verizon, Comcast, Huawei.

7. Energy and Utilities

- **Key Focus Areas:** Predictive maintenance, energy management, smart grids, demand forecasting.
- **Example Companies:** ExxonMobil, Chevron, Siemens, General Electric.

8. Manufacturing and Industry 4.0

- **Key Focus Areas:** Predictive maintenance, quality control, supply chain optimization, robotics and automation.
- **Example Companies:** Siemens, General Electric, Honeywell, Bosch.

9. Logistics and Supply Chain

- **Key Focus Areas:** Route optimization, demand forecasting, inventory management, autonomous delivery systems.
- **Example Companies:** FedEx, UPS, DHL, Amazon Logistics.

10. Entertainment and Media

- **Key Focus Areas:** Content recommendation, audience analytics, automated content creation, personalized advertising.
- **Example Companies:** Netflix, Disney, WarnerMedia, Spotify.

11. Government and Defense

- **Key Focus Areas:** National security, surveillance, public safety, data analysis.

- **Example Organizations:** Defense Advanced Research Projects Agency (DARPA), National Security Agency (NSA), various defense contractors.

12. Education and EdTech

- **Key Focus Areas:** Personalized learning, educational content creation, administrative automation, student performance analytics.
- **Example Companies:** Coursera, Khan Academy, Pearson, Duolingo.

13. Real Estate and PropTech

- **Key Focus Areas:** Property management, predictive maintenance, market analysis, smart buildings.
- **Example Companies:** Zillow, Redfin, Opendoor, CBRE.

These industries recognize the value of AI in transforming their operations, enhancing efficiency, and providing innovative solutions to complex problems. As a result, they are actively seeking AI Technical Program Managers to lead and manage AI initiatives.